D1616772

THE PEOPLE

PREHISTORIC NORTH AMERICA

THE PEOPLE

ROBERT PICKERING
ILLUSTRATED BY TED FINGER

THE MILLBROOK PRESS ■ BROOKFIELD, CONNECTICUT

TO THE MEMORY OF MISS MARY V. BLACK,
WHO THOUGHT THAT SCIENTISTS
ALSO SHOULD WRITE FOR CHILDREN.

Library of Congress Cataloging-in-Publication Data
Pickering, Robert B.
The people / by Robert B. Pickering ; illustrated by Ted Finger.
p. cm.—(Prehistoric North America)
Includes bibliographical references (p.) and index.
Summary: The story of prehistoric North Americans:
theories about when Paleo-Indians came, how they lived,
and how ways of life evolved over time.
ISBN 1-56294-550-5 (lib. bdg.)
1. Indians of North America—Antiquities—Juvenile literature.
2. Paleo-Indians—Juvenile literature. 3. North America—
Antiquities—Juvenile literature. [1. Indians of North America—
Origin. 2. Indians of North America—Antiquities. 3. Man,
Prehistoric. 4. North America—Antiquities.] I. Finger, Ted, ill.
II. Title. III. Series.
E77.92.P53 1995
973.01—dc20 95-3046 CIP AC

Published by The Millbrook Press, Inc.
2 Old New Milford Road, Brookfield, Connecticut 06804

6 5 4 3 2 1

250 MILLION YEARS AGO
the Triassic Period began. The animals of this period were primitive two-legged meat eaters.

208 MILLION YEARS AGO
the Jurassic Period (the Age of Dinosaurs) began. Sauropods—gigantic animals with long necks and small heads—were plant eaters who walked on four legs.

145 MILLION YEARS AGO
the Cretaceous Period began. Plant-eating armored and horned dinosaurs fought for survival with meat-eating giants.

65 MILLION YEARS AGO
the dinosaurs were gone. The Age of Mammals began. Early placentals evolved into the ancestors of the modern horse.

37 MILLION YEARS AGO
the creodonts (early meat-eating mammals) began to give way to the carnivores, such as the tree-climbing dawn dog, whose descendents include wolves, coyotes, and modern dogs.

2 MILLION YEARS AGO
during the Ice Age, huge, hearty animals such as wooly mammoths lived in large numbers near the glaciers of what is now Canada and the northern United States.

12,000 YEARS AGO
human beings followed herds of animals across the Bering Land Bridge into North America.

The People

Spring has come to the river valleys east of the Mississippi River. It is still too early in the year to find plant foods such as nuts, seeds, and greens. The snow has melted, though, and the great rivers—the Mississippi, the Ohio, and the Tennessee—have swelled and spread out over the floodplains. Smaller rivers and streams are also running fast. Ducks, geese, and swans are migrating north. As the waters rise, animals that cannot swim are forced out of the river valleys and up to higher ground.

This is the beginning of a rich season. Hunters prepare large nets and attach stone weights at equal distances around the edges. Before sunrise a few stealthy hunters sneak up on a flock of ducks sleeping on the floodwaters. When the men are as close as they dare, they throw the weighted nets over the unsuspecting ducks. It is a good catch, and the day is still young.

These hunters were living in what is now the eastern United States thousands of years ago. They lived in what we call prehistory, before the invention of writing. They were nomads, who followed the animals they hunted, such as elk, deer, and bison. People did not build permanent houses at this early time. They did build or find temporary shelter in cold, wet weather, though. They might come upon a dry cave or rock shelter. In warmer weather, they might put together a small lean-to or hut for protection from the damp.

By about 7,000 years ago, the weather across North America had become very much as it is today. Some parts of the country were cold and wet, other parts were hot and rainy, and still others were hot and dry. The different climates brought a great variety of plants and animals to the continent.

Wherever these early people, called Paleo-Indians, lived, they learned about the plants and animals around them. They knew which trees yielded a great harvest of nuts, which grasses produced tasty and abundant seeds, and where to find good water and safe places to rest and sleep at night.

DIGGING INTO THE PAST

How do we know that people lived in North America this long ago? After all, they left no written records for us to read. They did leave another kind of record. They left us physical clues. When we study the objects that prehistoric people left behind, a picture begins to take shape. We learn where people lived, how they hunted and fished for food, what kinds of plants they gathered in the woods and grasslands, the types of shelters they built, and even what they believed.

Early hunters using
a net to catch ducks.

Scientists who study ancient peoples and cultures are called archaeologists. The word culture describes how people lived and what beliefs they shared. Historians study human cultures, too, but usually they look at cultures or countries with written languages.

Archaeologists "read" objects, just as historians read the words left behind in books. Reading an object, or artifact, means examining it to learn about how it was used and about the people who made it. Archaeologists are detectives who try to answer questions about the past through clues left at the scene. They excavate, or dig, artifacts out of the ground that were left there by our human ancestors. Any object made by human hands is an artifact. A stone spear point, a ceramic pot, a bicycle, even this book that you are holding are all artifacts of human culture.

Artifacts are usually found at places, called sites, where people used them. A site might be an entire Mayan city grown over by the jungle. It might be the wreck of a Roman ship at the bottom of the Mediterranean Sea. It might also be a spot on the plains of Colorado where a single person who made one spear point left stone chips behind.

Until about 1920, archaeologists had found no Paleo-Indian sites. They had found many Paleo-Indian spear points, though. These were very thin and sharp and often made from beautiful materials—all marks of master craftsmen.

One of the most important Paleo-Indian sites was found by accident. In the 1920s an African-American cowboy named George McJunkin was riding near Folsom, New Mexico, along a washed-out stream bank. McJunkin saw bones sticking out of the dirt. After a close look at them, he knew that they were neither horse nor cow bones.

Eventually, Jesse Figgins, curator at the Denver Museum of Natural History, heard about McJunkin's find. Figgins was a university-trained archaeologist—a rare person at the time. He agreed that McJunkin had found something very important. He also knew that if his hunch was correct—that this was a very old site—he would need proof that would stand up to the scrutiny of the best scientists of the day. So Figgins assembled a team of experienced excavators and a geologist, who knew all about dating the age of rocks, and they started digging.

The cowboy and the archaeologist had made a real find. They uncovered the first North American site in which human tools were found among the bones of extinct Ice Age bison! Unusual stone spear points were among the partly fossilized ribs (that is, the bones had begun to turn into stone). This discovery proved that people had been in North America at the end of the Ice Age, at least 10,000 to 12,000 years ago.

The Folsom find changed the way scientists saw America's past.

THE FIRST IMMIGRANTS

The ancestors of all human beings who live on this continent came from somewhere else. We are all immigrants. But until the Folsom find, we had no idea how long ago the first people came here. In fact, the time of their arrival is still a big question. We know that people were here by the end of the Ice Age, which lasted from about 2 million to 12,000 years ago. People may have migrated to North America during this time. And groups may have arrived here from different places at different times.

Here is the most widely accepted theory about when and how people came: Scientists know that during the Ice Age winters were longer, snow was heavier, and the short summers did not always thaw the ice. Over thousands of years, great glaciers built up around the far north. As more and more of the Earth's water was frozen into glacial ice, the sea level fell. Lower sea level meant that more land was exposed along the coasts of continents and islands.

The Americas are closest to Eurasia at the edge of the Bering Strait. About 14,000 to 12,000 years ago, water covering the strait had receded, and a broad marshy extension of land connected Siberia and North America. This land is called the Bering Land Bridge.

Paleontologists, who examine the skeletons of ancient animals, have shown that during the Ice Age

During the Ice Age, bison, mastodons, and wild horses were among the animals that crossed the Bering Land Bridge into North America.

the kinds of animals in Siberia and the northern reaches of North America were the same. There were mammoths, mastodons, wild horses, musk-oxen, and bison. There were also giant meat eaters—short-faced bears, lions, and wolves—who hunted other animals. About 12,000 years ago, another species of hunter—human beings—followed the herds across the land bridge. These early immigrants moved south.

This southern migration leads to more questions. People moved south from Alaska to at least as far as Mexico in about 1,500 years. This might seem like a long time, but in terms of human history it is not. Scientists wonder how people moved this far south so fast without horses, much less any kind of wheeled vehicle.

Recent discoveries in South America have complicated things even more. Paleo sites have been found that may be 10,000 years older than sites in North America. If the first Americans came across the Bering Land Bridge, how could this be?

Many ideas have been suggested. People might have come from Siberia, not at the end of the Ice Age but sometime during the Ice Age. Or ancient Phoenicians, Egyptians, West Africans, Pacific Islanders, and Japanese might have also landed in the Americas. There is very little evidence to support these ideas, but scientists still wonder.

There *is* evidence of a much more recent settlement. A Viking site called L'Anse aux Meadows lies on the cold northeastern shore of Canada. It dates from about A.D. 1,000. The Vikings seem to have met with hostile people in the region and abandoned their village. Other people might also have come here but stayed only a short time.

We are certain about one thing. Christopher Columbus was not the first person to set foot on this continent. After his arrival, everything changed, though. Europeans brought writing with them to North America. They also brought different ways of life. In time, the cultures of the prehistoric people who had been here for thousands of years either died out or were greatly changed.

PALEO-INDIAN WAYS OF LIFE

We know that between 12,000 and 9,000 years ago, early hunters were living and hunting in areas now known as Colorado, New Mexico, Illinois, and Pennsylvania. Their special spear points, called fluted points, have been found throughout the United States. At some sites, such as Folsom in New Mexico and Dent in Colorado, fluted points were found with the remains of extinct animals. At the Meadowcroft rock shelter in Pennsylvania, an actual site was excavated where Paleo-Indians once camped.

In just a few thousand years, people had spread across Canada, the United States, and at least as far south as Mexico.

After the glaciers retreated, much of what had been forests was replaced by grasslands.

These people were living just after the end of the last Ice Age. North America's climate became warmer and drier, the great glaciers retreated, and the sea level rose. Whatever immigrant plants and animals had spread to America were now permanent residents. Where ancient lush forests had once covered much of North America, the new climate forced the forests to recede. They were replaced by marshy ground covered with thick grass and a few sparse trees. These grasslands became the Midwestern prairies of today.

This change in climate and plants had a big effect on animals. Many large plant-eating animals (herbivores) evolved—that is, they changed gradually to survive. Other herbivores became extinct, or died out completely.

By 9,000 years ago, most of the large plant eaters—mammoths, mastodons, musk-oxen, camels, and horses—were gone. Only the great shaggy bison survived into modern times.

HUNTERS ▪ Some archaeologists think that early humans may have hunted mammoths and mastodons to extinction.

At many sites in the American West, the bones of these ancient relatives of modern elephants have been found along with human-made hunting tools. Sometimes their bones show evidence of butchering marks.

Hunters with primitive weapons
surround a huge mammoth.

Hunting mammoths and mastodons must have been dangerous. These animals were big, fast, and strong. Big bulls may have weighed as much as 14,000 pounds (6,300 kilograms) and stood 12 feet (3.7 meters) high. Their size made them dangerous. It also made them a huge store of meat for early hunters.

Mammoth hunters used very simple weapons. The hunters were smart, though. They knew the animals' behavior and the terrain in which they lived. Hunters worked in groups to stalk these big animals. It is highly probable that the hunters selected their prey carefully and then set up ambushes to trap them.

Many parts of North America show evidence that Paleo-Indians hunted bison herds as well. The bison (buffalo) of this time were much larger than the ones we know. They stood a foot taller and had larger horns. Big bulls may have weighed up to 3,000 pounds (1,350 kilograms) and been about the size of a small car. Today, a large Hereford or Charolais bull weighs only about 2,000 pounds (900 kilograms).

Nomadic Families ▪ Archaeologists think that these hunters traveled in small family groups of about twenty to twenty-five people. The band might include a father, mother, their daughters, the daughters' husbands, and their children. When men married, it is likely that they moved out of their own family and into their wife's family group.

Families set up camps wherever the hunting was good.

The elder men and women guided the younger members of the group. The younger men and women did the hard work of hunting, making tools and clothing, and providing for the needs of the entire group. Even the children probably helped to gather edible plants, firewood, and the other things needed to set up camp. Some plants were for food, but others would be used for medicine or to turn into string, rope, or bags for carrying things.

Along with their mothers, daughters probably helped butcher and cook the meat for the whole group. Girls learned to make the tools they would need in their work. They also cared for the younger children. Boys learned to observe the habits of animals, to hunt, and to make hunting equipment.

The things people owned were few and simple but very important. As nomads, it would be too much trouble to have many possessions. Anything you owned, you had to carry. However, at some places, tools were left for future use. Harvest sites have been discovered in places where an abundance of seeds or nuts were found. People would search out a large flat rock and a smaller round one. The small rock, the right size to fit the hand, would be the hammer stone for cracking nuts. On the large flat stone, seeds were ground into flour. These stones were left at the harvest site because they were too heavy to carry, and besides, they were only needed in the place where the nuts and seeds were found.

Weapons and Tools ▪ Men made their own hunting tools.

Seven thousand years ago, the most common weapons were the spear and atlatl, or spear thrower.

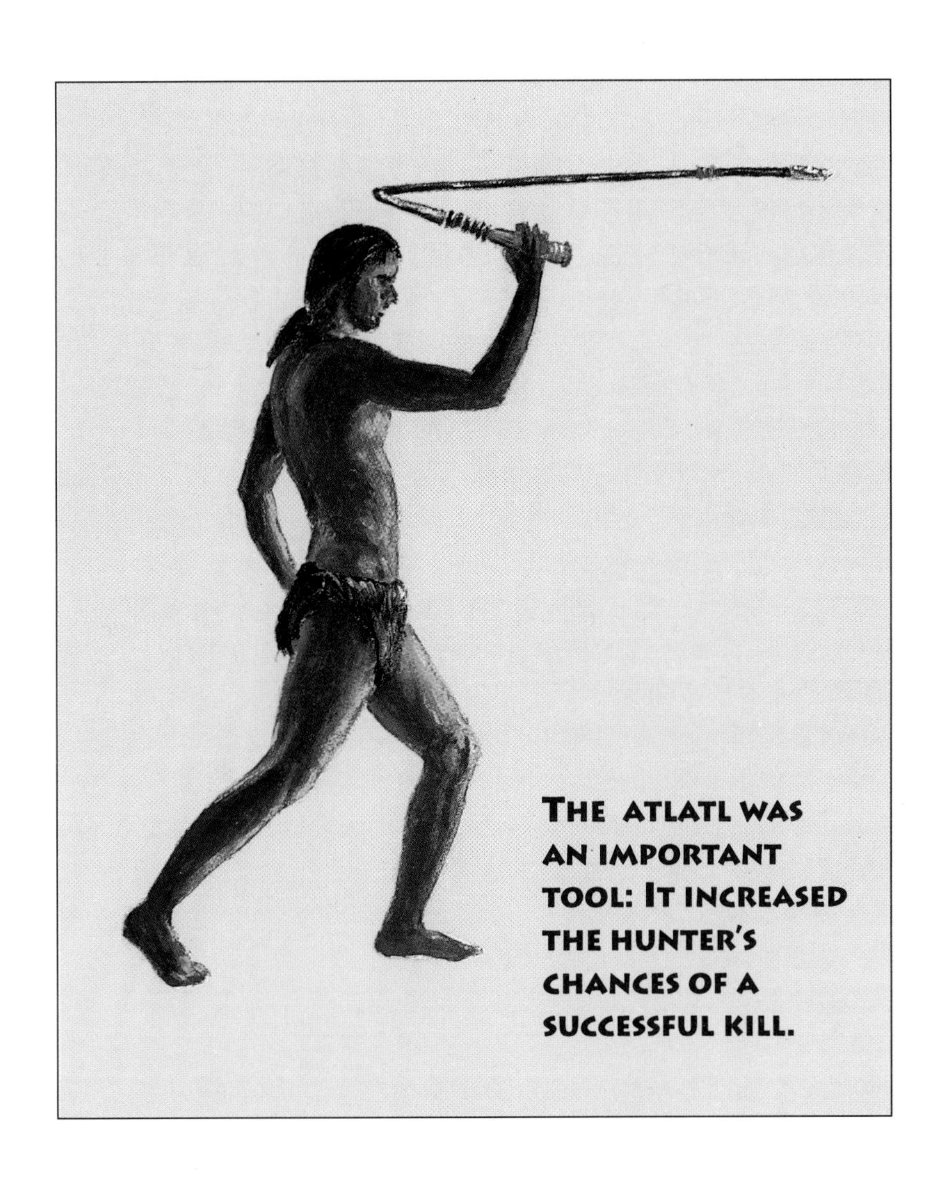

The atlatl was an important tool: It increased the hunter's chances of a successful kill.

An atlatl is a simple but very powerful device. It is a rather narrow, flattened piece of wood that has been carefully smoothed and shaped. On one end is the handle for holding. On the other end is a notch or a hook into which the thrower places the end of his spear. There may also be a weight or stone attached to the atlatl shaft to improve its balance.

The atlatl allowed hunters to throw their spears much farther and harder without losing any accuracy. Spear points were chipped out of stone. The combination of a sharp stone point, a spear thrower, and the strong arm of a hunter was the main method of providing meat for thousands of years.

Paleo-Indian points stopped being used about 9,000 years ago. Gone are the beautiful, long fluted points that were used to hunt the great mammoth, the mastodon, and the Ice Age bison. Gone, too, are those very animals. However, the people survived.

SURVIVAL AND CHANGE

Between 10,000 years ago and the arrival of Christopher Columbus only 500 years ago, ways of life for Paleo-Indians and their descendants changed in many ways. Over that long period of time, the human population continued to grow. More people required more food. The old way of hunting over large territories was no longer practical. Family bands began to stay in one region. The people learned the landforms, the types of plants, and the habits of animals within their region very well. As archaeologists say, they began to be specialists.

The survival of prehistoric people was tied directly to the climate, plants, and animals around them. This means that ways of life differed a great deal in the hot, dry Southwest, in the cooler climate of the East, and along the rainy, temperate Northwest Coast. Let's look now at how these early people lived in different parts of North America.

In the Southwestern Deserts ▪ Peoples of the deserts of the American Southwest—in the present-day states of Utah, Nevada, California, Colorado, Arizona, and New Mexico—lived in small family bands. They hunted animals and gathered the plants that grew in their dry environment. Deer, wild pigs, and sheep, and smaller animals such as rabbits, mice, birds and their eggs provided meat and protein. These people learned to pick the fruit of the prickly pear cactus. They not only ate the fruit but also learned to crush and preserve the seeds. They collected the nuts of the piñon pine and the seeds of wild grasses.

Some parts of the Southwest were not quite as dry, although water was still scarce. People hunted there, but they also began to experiment with a new way of life: farming. By 3,000 years ago, gourds, squash, and beans were all raised for food. The gourds were also made into light and strong containers, used to hold anything from water to seeds. The seeds of gourds and squash were preserved and eaten.

Along with the seeds of gourds and squash came the knowledge of how to plant them. Knowledge of astronomy and some religious ideas spread north from Mexico. Although we do not often think of it, all farmers are astronomers. They need a basic knowledge of the sun, moon, seasons, and climate. They need to be able to predict the seasons and to know when the rains will come. They must decide on the best time to plant.

Through farming, for the first time in human history in America, people learned how to control their own food supply.

Also about 3,000 years ago, people began to cultivate corn. For nearly a thousand years, corn was a less important food than beans. Eventually, it became the most important plant crop in North America. Though not a food crop, cotton was grown by about 1,200 years ago. Cotton was probably used for making clothing, which had been made in earlier days from animal hides.

Like farmers all over the world, the Indians of the Southwest learned that to have a good harvest they had to settle in one place to cultivate and protect their plants. At first, they might have lived in rock shelters. They preferred to live facing south so that they were exposed to the winter sun and had warm places to work and to talk and rest at the end of the day.

The early farmers of the Southwest learned another important lesson. Crops do not grow without water.

The farmers picked areas of good soil near streams and rivers to plant crops. As time went on, their fields extended into drier areas thanks to an important invention: irrigation. By working together, the Southwestern farmers built canals to channel the runoff from snow melting at higher elevations to their plots. Once the irrigation canals were built, they had to be maintained. People worked together to make sure that the system held up.

Over the next few thousand years, the population of the Southwest grew. Farming replaced hunting and gathering as the main way to survive. People no longer lived in simple rock shelters. They built huge stone apartment houses. Sometimes hundreds of rooms with high ceilings were built in one large D shape. Among the living rooms were rooms for storing and grinding corn. There were also special places called kivas. These round rooms, which were partly underground, were used for religious purposes. The walls of these sacred rooms were decorated with paintings of sacred events, spiritual beings, and religious stories about the past.

"Apartment houses" perched atop cliffs in the Southwest desert.

IN THE BOUNTIFUL EAST ▪ East of the Mississippi River, the early hunters and gatherers lived in a world rich in plant and animal life. The many rivers in the eastern United States were very important for food and transportation. In the rivers were fish, turtles, and shellfish. In the spring and fall, the great rivers were temporary homes to millions of migrating ducks, geese, and swans. The flood basins of the rivers also produced a variety of animals and many kinds of edible plants.

Food of many kinds was plentiful and nutritious. The animals and the plants and land offered the necessities and even the luxuries of life. People wore animal skins to keep warm during the cold, wet winters. Marsh grasses were woven into mats for covering houses or into baskets for carrying goods. People made many kinds of tools out of flint and stone. They beat copper nuggets into finc tools and beautiful ornaments. Important people wore freshwater pearls on their robes. Pearls, copper artifacts, and other objects were sometimes traded to distant people in exchange for local artifacts or stones.

Hunting and gathering continued to be important. About 1,100 years ago, the bow and arrow was introduced. Hunters could then shoot animals at greater distances. The bow and arrow was a better weapon than the spear and atlatl. The deadly arrows had smaller stone points that could be made more quickly than the larger spear points.

As the population grew and people began to live closer together, food became less plentiful. People began to compete for the shrinking hunting grounds. Sometimes they fought. There is evidence that for the first time in North America people were killing other people. In some burial sites, human skeletons have been found with arrow heads embedded in their bones.

EASTERN WOODLAND PEOPLES OF ABOUT 1,100 YEARS AGO USED BOWS AND ARROWS TO HUNT.

About 1,100 years ago, people began to farm as well as to hunt and gather. Because food became abundant again, populations grew large. Some towns, such as Cahokia near the city of East St. Louis, may have had thousands of people living in a city surrounded by a wooden wall. The houses of great rulers and the shrines of the ancestors were built on huge earthen mounds inside the city. During the year, farmers went out from the cities to tend their crops, or they lived in small houses near their fields during the growing season.

There were many other big towns and cities besides Cahokia. Aztalan in Wisconsin, Etowah in Georgia, Chucalissa in Alabama, and Spiro in Oklahoma were all large cities and centers for ceremonies. Each of these sites was built on good fertile soil, usually near the intersection of two major rivers. Most of these sites were also surrounded by wooden stockades, probably for defense.

Over time, a ruling class developed. Leadership was passed on through families—that is, it was hereditary. While most of the paintings and drawings show men dressed in official robes, there are also pictures of women. These women might have been the ancestors of the ruling families. Or perhaps they were the fertility goddesses that these farming people prayed to.

There were warriors who wore magnificent clothing and ornaments to show their importance to others. There may have been a class of traders who

In the city of Cahokia, near present-day East St. Louis, thousands of people may have lived in houses atop large earthen mounds.

were always looking for new sources of the stone, shell, and other materials that were used to make symbols of status and power for the ruling class.

These great cities of the East were spectacular. About 800 years ago, however, nearly 300 years before Columbus landed, most of the great cities were abandoned.

Perhaps the large, densely packed populations damaged their environment so that farming no longer produced enough food. Perhaps epidemic disease such as tuberculosis made the cities unhealthy places to live. There may have been political and religious strife. Archaeologists are not certain why the cities fell into ruin. Probably all of these reasons, and possibly other ones too, led to the fall of the mounded cities.

ALONG THE RAINY NORTHWEST COAST ▪ The area along the coasts of Oregon, Washington, British Columbia (Canada), and Alaska is now called the Northwest Coast. Unlike the Southwest, this region had a heavy rainfall. The great forests were lush and tall. They were almost too lush. The trees were large and grew close together. Other plants were squeezed out, so that fewer kinds of plants and animals made their homes there.

Numerous islands dotted the coast, and many small fingers of land stretched out into the Pacific Ocean. There were quiet bays, large beaches, and easy access to the deep forests by way of rivers and streams.

The lush forests and the richness of the sea offered plenty of food to the people of this region. They hunted sea mammals and fished. From their small villages along the coast and at the mouths of rivers, they used harpoons to kill seals and the smaller species of whales. They fished with hooks, nets, and spears.

From early times, salmon appears to have been a very important food in this region. Salmon was dried or smoked to preserve it for the winter. By at least 3,000 years ago, people learned that the salmon always came back to the rivers from the sea at certain times of the year. If they had their nets and spears ready, a small family group of men, women, and children could catch and preserve a lot of fish in a very short time.

Just as they learned about the migration of salmon, people living along the coast and near rivers learned about the movements of seals, whales, ducks, geese, and other wild animals. They ate cod, herring, halibut, and rockfish. Women and children collected clams.

By 2,000 years ago, ways of life existed that are still part of the culture of Northwest Coast tribes today. Part of that life is based on the kinds of wild game that abound there and the ways they are hunted. Some rivers had bigger salmon runs than

Fishing along the Northwest Coast on the Olympic Peninsula.

others. Some parts of the river were easier to fish. There were stretches of beach that were more protected places to live than others. Families or clans claimed choice sites and defended them against other people. Some of these claims still hold today.

A natural disaster created a time capsule of life along the Northwest Coast. On a day about 400 years ago, a huge mudslide buried at least four houses at the site of Ozette on the Olympic Peninsula. Everything inside was sealed off. The fine, wet mud preserved many things that usually are destroyed by time and the environment. At Ozette, thousands of wooden, fiber, and fabric artifacts were found. Almost all of them were just as they had been left.

Archaeologists could see how these people built their cedar plank houses. They found benches inside the houses that were used for sitting and sleeping. Artifacts that were clustered together have been identified as the gear of seal and whale hunters and the tools of woodworkers. Tools for preparing food, making clothing, and other domestic chores were found inside the houses.

There is also evidence of early city planning. Archaeologists have excavated a drainage system that channeled rainwater away from the houses and living areas. Clearly, these people had lived in their homes for a long time and expected that Ozette would be home long into the future. The mudslide ended that dream, but it recorded the great skill, cleverness, and wealth of the people of Ozette for all of us to know.

AN ONGOING STORY

The Paleo-Indians were the first people to come to the Americas. Their descendants are still here. They make up the many tribes of Indians that live in North America today. Many of those who survived the arrival of Europeans live on reservations. Others live in cities across the country. In some ways, their lives are no different from those of their ancestors. There is still a deep respect for nature and a belief that all life and the Earth itself is sacred and connected. Some of the ancient sacred rituals are still performed today. It is likely that many tribal stories passed on from parents to children today were told by elders to young people thousands of years ago. Old traditions have not died.

At the same time, modern life affects all of us, Indian or not. Many Indians have the same kinds of jobs, houses, and clothes as their non-Indian neighbors. They go to school, drive cars, and listen to the same music as many other people do. Yet they keep their traditions alive. Sometimes it is hard to live in both worlds. Other times, it is an advantage to be able to live in the old and the new. Perhaps that is why Indian cultures have survived for so long.

Timeline

Years Ago:

2 million	The Ice Age begins.
14,000	The Bering Land Bridge forms.
12,000	The Ice Age ends.
9,000	Mammoths, mastodons, musk-oxen, camels, and horses have died out in North America.
3,000	Mexican-Indian farmers are growing corn, gourds, squash, and beans.
1,100	Cahokia is the largest city in North America. The bow and arrow is a common hunting weapon in the East.
1,000	The Vikings build a settlement in northeastern Canada.
800	Cahokia and many of the great cities are abandoned.
500	Christopher Columbus arrives in the West Indies, and the flow of Europeans to North America begins.
400	The Ozette site is buried in a large mudslide.

Find Out More

The Ancient Cliff Dwellers of Mesa Verde, by Caroline Arnold (Boston: Houghton Mifflin, 1992).

Explore the World of Prehistoric Life, by Dougal Dixon (New Bern, N.C.: Western Publishers, 1992).

Prehistoric Life, by Steve Parker (New York: Dorling Kindersley, 1993).

Prehistoric People, by Laurence Santrey (New York: Troll Associates, 1985).

Stones and Bones! How Archaeologists Trace Human Origins, by Avraham Ronen (Minneapolis: Lerner Publications, 1993).

INDEX

Page numbers in *italics* refer to illustrations.

About the Author

Robert B. Pickering's passion to learn about the people and cultures of the past began when he was a child. His interest in our ancient human ancestors led him to participate in archaeological excavations in many parts of the world, including the American Midwest, north and west Mexico, the Island of Yap, and Thailand. Dr. Pickering has written many scientific articles, but in the past few years he has written several books for children and edited two series of anthropological children's books.